Traces of Wonder

Poems
Of life
And loss
And pebbles on the shoreline
Where they cross

JOHN TRIMMER

ISBN: 9798410174213

Traces

Sketches,
Light lines loosely filling in the edges
Of truths we think we see around ourselves,
Rough words penciled in,
Crossed out, changed, and rearranged,
To capture shades of where our wonder delves.

We feel out threads of life and loss
And listen to the wisdom they impart.
Do you see them, where they cross –
Traces of a greater truth at heart?

CONTENTS

PRELUDE

POEMS

A Poet's Process

I don't know how others do it.
Do they take in each word and chew it
Until its shape is solid in the mind?
And then, do they construct a shell
Of words that fit together well,
Before they choose a structure meant to bind
The similes and metaphors
That float above uncertain shores
With grounded truths in layers well-refined?
In me, some unknown combination
Of searching, struggle, and inspiration
Moves my pen through patterns less defined.
I can't decipher, when I dare,
How through the process I am driven,
But I am glad to humbly share
What words this grace has given.

Repetition

There is an art to repetition,
Which may escape my efforts still.
Too much at once, and all will feel
Like hammer blows and overkill.
The droning of such exposition
Is circling like the turning of a wheel,
So I must search for something new,
But novelty must build on something real.
The premise of this proposition –
Do you feel it's true?
Do we find our greatest skill
When the past imparts a view
Of the future's unknown expedition?
What lessons do our steps reveal
For walking forth toward untouched paths that heal?

Below the Surface

For some, it flows like water
Or wine from out of crystal jars.
Their words set hearts aflutter
And glitter like the sparkling stars.
My own attempts are struggles
To draw out thoughts from in my mind.
I mumble, pause, and stutter.
Internal gears that slip and grind
Grow somehow ever louder,
Cause any dreams of erudition
To dwindle, fall, and sputter,
And always force a recognition
That each word needs rehearsing.
Yet even preparatory passes
Do not remove the feeling
Of pulling thoughts through thick molasses
Before they reach the light.
Now, is it clearer why I write
And form my phrases first with ink?
It gives me space to stop and think.
The pen will wait, will give me time
Even to find a fitting rhyme
For some far deeper notion
That flows below the surface of an ever-shifting ocean.

The Book that Sleeps Beside My Head

When lifting up the mosquito net
And climbing into bed,
I bring with me a notebook that
Will sleep beside my head.

It lies upon my pillow while
My thoughts explore the stores of night
To search through each poetic vial
And find what words to write.

Yet if I do, it seems more true
That you've inspired the dreams which guide my sight.

Embodying Emotion

The words do not come cheaply
When writing of emotion.
The poet feels it deeply,
Embodying each notion,
Then lining up some rhymes that fit
The currents of its ocean.

Projection, make-believe, or empathy,
I'm not sure what to make of it,
But each imagined life that comes to me,
Regardless, teaches me a bit
Of joys and pains and wonder,
And I must hold them deeply
To heal or rend my heart asunder,
But the price is felt less steeply
If the words reach someone, somewhere
And embody depths for them to share.

PART 1

OF LIFE

First Steps Away

To see her run and jump and fall
And hone her skills
Until she stands before you, tall
And ready to begin
To scale the closest rolling hills
And feel the warmth upon her skin
Where sunlight floods the sky,
And then to seek for greater thrills
Beyond the paths that wander nigh
Toward faraway vast mountain-scapes
Where water falls unbroken, spills
Upon the rocks in frothy shapes,
And makes her dreams come true,
Her searching spirit, soaring, fills
Your watchful eyes with what her future holds in view.

To Turn at the Crossroads

I come to a fork in the road through the wood,
And a choice must be made where to go.
Running right, left, and straight are the options. What good
Will evolve from the footprints I'll grow?

Staying straight is perhaps the easiest way
For the moment, at least, but again,
Quite quickly, I'll meet a new crossroads and may
Face greater uncertainty then.
The straight path leads toward what I thought I desire,
A distant white tower ahead
Beckons onward, but pitfalls exist and inspire
A turn to a second thread.

On the right, climbing fast to a tall, airy peak,
I would soon leave the woodland behind.
The view extends far, and the voices that speak
May reach many with new thoughts aligned.
It's a path I knew not, when starting my course,
But revealed, it presents some exciting
And broad possibilities, close to my source,
Though a soft voice inside me is fighting.

I finally look to the left, which slopes down
To a faraway plain where the trees
Grow thick, bearing fruit from a leafy green gown,
And the warm waters run with the breeze.
While I can't see the future, there may be a chance
To return to the road I've been on
If it calls, but for now, this elongated glance
Just feels right. To the left I am drawn.

It's unknown, but familiar – far away, yet near
To some places I've walked before.
And the longer I look, something seems to appear:
It's my heart, my passion, my core.

Grown Again

The fallen seed was newly born
And sprouted through the soil toward the sun,
But soon it stretched too far, too fast,
Collapsing when expanding clouds had won
The sky.

Years passed until the present morn
When, once again, the life of days gone by
Returns to grow again and cast
Its gaze to capture sunshine's warm supply
Of light.

But now, more sturdy branches run
And spread more slowly to a humble height.
Imperfect yet, the rising stem will try
To stand
Through any storm or chill of night.

Days Spent Sailing on the Sea

Day one
Was met by rising sun,
And worries were so very few –
An easy course to run.

Day two,
The storm came into view,
Too large to turn the boat and flee,
I started plunging through.

Day three
Was hardest yet for me.
I lost all sight of any shore
While rain was falling free.

Day four,
The waves were rising more,
And, every crest, the boat would strive
To cross perdition's door.

Day five
I'd kept myself alive.
The storm had passed, but, with that fix,
More struggles would derive.

Day six
Brought sunlight, playing tricks.
I'd lost my course through earth and heaven
In storm wind's swirling mix.

Day seven
Passed through to day eleven,
When, in a daze, I spotted land
And found the strength to stand.

Those days spent sailing on the sea
Diverged from what I thought they'd be,

But now I try, upon the sand,
To learn the truths revealed to me.

Money

A construct –
Cleverly conceived, indeed –
Assigning value to the things
We make and want and need.
Created as a way to trade
Across so many types of things –
Products, skills, an education,
And melodies a singer sings –
Its use inflated to pertain
To nearly every realm of life.
Has it become too much revered,
Too much a cold, abstracted knife
That separates us each from each?
We place much stock in shreds of paper,
Assigning numbers to our worth.
We see salvation, climbing higher,
Until our interests crash to Earth.
The bubbles burst,
And suddenly all chaos reigns.
It's dangerous, this thirst
For growth at any cost. The gains
Are less than true. It's all a construct –
A means to let our varied skills
Take flight – but it's become an end:
A number that this world distills
To measure who is worthy.
We made it up,
But now it lines each strand of thought
And rattles in each beggar's cup.
Yet life holds so much more
Than cash flows on a balance sheet.
Each being far surpasses
This cold invention. More complete,
We stand upon the Earth and sing
With bodies, souls, and selves
More wonderful than any coin
Can say.

The human spirit delves
For gold far greater than we buy
Or sell or save or lend,
And always, holy ground is nigh
To raise us toward a better end.
If only we could see it
More clearly than our pride and greed
For things that dissipate to nothing
Beyond an artificial seed.
A construct –
Cleverly conceived, indeed –
Does not define the sacred strings
With which our lives are bound and freed,
And it should not constrain the things
That those at risk most dearly need.

Abiding

Yesterday, I stood
With the screen door open wide
To feel the world I'm distanced from
And all the unacknowledged good
It holds. I stood a bit inside,
Took in the air, and heard the hum
Of growing things that sprout and crawl and glide.
In the end, I thought of you
And knew
Your presence will abide.

The World at the Window

The scent of the rain,
The touch of the breeze
Protect me from the daily strain
Of isolation's draining freeze.
The sound of a bird,
The sight of the sun
Uplift my soul without a word,
Forgive me for what's left undone.
A taste of life's expanse
Connects me, where my body stands,
To all the world's varied dance,
To you in near and distant lands.

Sitting Out as the Sun Goes Down

After returning from a run
And showering off the sweat,
I take a folding chair outside
Upon the deck and let
Myself recline beneath the angled sun.
Preoccupied by data shining
From the computer upon my lap,
I do a little work, defining
Trends before my sightlines snap
And look around.
The orange sphere's descended,
A stillness settles on the ground,
The sky has purpled and extended
To meet the full moon's pale and yellow light,
And I return inside, refreshed
By the magical turning of day to night.

Upon the Balcony

I sit upon the balcony,
A drink is at my side,
And read the words of fantasy
That other authors wrote to guide
My mind to other places
Fictional and filled with faces
Different from my own.
But also, glancing toward the sky,
I watch the sun descend its throne
And cast its final rays on high
To fill the cloudy spaces,
Covering the gray with traces
Tinged with multicolored light.
Whether read or seen,
These evening moments lift my sight
To find the hidden, sacred sheen
Of this world's many graces.
Nightfall swiftly primes its paces,
Words and shades made one, with me, serene.

Walking After Dark

There's something about walking after dark
When the air is cool and the shadows stark
Below the periodic streetlamps' glow.
A special magic percolates, its mark
Drapes itself over every unseen arc
Where searching souls and spirits grow
To bind the threads that make the world one.
Or maybe I'm simply homeward bound
As the night sky's crowned and the day is done.

A Sliver of the Sun

A sliver of the sun
Given life by wick and wax
Flickers in a darkened room,
So fragile in the winds that run
But leave behind no tracks.
A flame against the gathered gloom
Guides the spirits of the night
Toward a space where tales are spun
And woven, finding all the cracks
That haunt the human heart, but bright
The stories build and bloom
To block each new nocturnal fright.

With time, wax dripping, dripping down
Dims the sinking candlelight,
But as the sliver starts to drown
And heavy eyeballs lose their sight,
There falls a new protective gown
Of stories sown by fire's gleam,
Which guards against the doldrums' bite
And grants a hopeful dream.

Were I to Dream Again this Dream

I'm standing on a grassy hill
Overlooking valleys green
And gazing at the skyward scene
Where the endless blues instill
A sense of unknown depths, marine
In their character and tone,
But hiding something all their own
Underneath the surface sheen.
Then suddenly an empty stone –
A darkened disk – obstructs the sun
And takes its time to slowly run
In front of all the light. Alone
It waits to see what work it's done
As floating balls of cooling light
Traverse the skies of midday night,
Purple-blue on dark, at one
With all the magic of this sight
Offered up within a dream
Where eyes can find what treasures seem
Impossible in waking flight.

Were I to dream again this dream,
I'd follow what the shadows show
Of lights that, in the darkness, grow
And grant us strength beneath their gleam.

Waking to a Sliver of the Moon

Rise today to greet the morn before the dawn
When skies are dark and stars are bright and streets are still,
As the city sleeps, still hot without the sun,
While memories of dreams before deflect the quill
Which writes of present day.
Like a freshly filed fingernail, austere,
A sliver of the moon appears without a flaw.
Almost all in shadow, lunar light shines clear.
What little of this world I've known, I stand in awe,
And so I hope to stay.

At Rest

"An object at rest remains at rest."
This (partial) first law of motion
Is the law of motion I know the best,
For while I lie in the slumbering ocean
Of early morning dreams, the dawn
Begins to dance through the windowpane
Beside my bed, and the conjured fawn
Begins to prance upon my sleeping brain,
But still I remain at rest.

I wait to rise, to wake, to test
My movements as the night transitions
To newborn day. My senses soon suggest
Resuming life's bold expeditions
Beyond the realms of dreaming,
But even in the sunlight's beaming,
Still I remain at rest.

Then, finally, the impulse of the spheres –
Forever revolving, marking time –
Compels me, as the image disappears,
To rise, to wake, to heed the chime
And cross the threshold into conscious rhyme.
Yet rest remains a natural state,
Returning nightly with unerring fate.

A Seasonal Anachronism

This order feels all wrong.
It's not been cold for very long,
But snow's already fallen on the ground.
The bottoms of the trees
Reflect a silent winter's sound,
But multicolored leafy canopies
Still rustle in an autumn breeze,
And, slowly, leaves are drifting down
To land upon the snow.
A graceful beauty's white and brown-flecked gown
Has warped the seasons' flow.
Its soft anachronism
Leaves my heart aglow
Yet fearful of a harder schism
We may unknowingly have crossed.
What if there's no returning
From where the seasons' rhythm is lost?
What changes will we still be learning
Long after all the harm we've wrought?
Perhaps they will be greater than we thought.

Whisper, Winter

Whisper, winter, where your winds will wander –
Over mountain, meadow, deep or shallow.
Whisper, wisdom, where the year will sunder,
Flames extinguished from the wick and tallow.
Every mile traversed will mark the marrow
Aching in the frigid cold, but follow
Every trial until the road will narrow,
Pointing toward the way where every hollow
Offers shelter from the winter storming.
Even when the snowy clouds are forming,
Somewhere else the slope of season's arrow
Points another way, and with the morning
Comes a warmer dawn of light adorning
Summer skies of sapphire blue. I wander
Through the splintered sights of seasons' turning.
Whisper, winter, cover summer's thunder,
Play your part in hearts' and climates' churning.

Like Tinsel Strung Around the World

Like tinsel strung around the world,
Spiraling from needled branch to star,
We glitter with transparent light
That transports us beyond horizons far.
Along these lines, we lift our sight
Across the oceans wide and mountains tall.
We're sewn together, somehow, in the squall.
It's not the same as what the past has brought,
But it's enough
To weather what this waning year has wrought.

Walk Along

Walk along
With the donkeys and the cattle and the goats
Where the votes
Cast across the sea by a stormy throng
Would seem at once remote
When parched is the throat and harsh is the note
Of bitter sand, swept sailing on the wind,
But links with mobile grazing herds
May grow with future leaders' words
If water's hold is further thinned.

Coming of Age

The ceremony came and went.
Did it make the world new?
They'd said the years he's thus far lent
Were now his own, to live and do
As he saw fit.
They'd said his lifetime would be split
Between the younger days he spent
As he was learning bit by bit
What being someone older meant,
And all the years
Beyond today, whose dawn holds fears
And hopes exceeding what he's knit
Before. He hears the ringing cheers
And wonders if this moment's lit
So differently.
He still believes that there will be
Greater dreams and stronger tears
Yet knows the truly crucial key
Is not the ceremony's gears
But how he lives the life he'll see.

Another Home Another Day

The red-brown *murram* road is running,
Cutting through the landscape filled with green,
From woody hills' horizons, stunning,
Basking in the sunlight's golden sheen,
To wetland lily pads and reeds
Leading toward a town of memories.
Each building, shop, and pathway bleeds
Into an image drawn from melodies
Of years gone by.
And all that I remember
Comes rushing back, and as the visions fly,
I think of what you said that last November
When I flew off to find another home
But promised to return another day.
To paraphrase: No matter where I roam,
A part of me would always stay
With you, beneath the leaves of *ffene* trees.
In every other home that knows my gaze,
I hope I leave some blessing on the breeze.

Tightrope Crawlers

They scamper along the top of a wall,
Then wait their turn on a faded church sign
To cross the street on an overhead line,
Being careful not to fall.

Their light brown fur is standing on end
With tails outstretched, adjusting their balance.
It's a privilege to witness such samples of talents
In these years of life I spend.

A hand or foot, on occasion, may slip,
But they stay atop the electrical cable.
Their remaining appendages keep themselves stable
As what faltered finds it grip.

And once they have bravely attained the far side,
I wonder what crossings my caution and fear have denied.

City and Savanna

Standing here
On the boundary between
The world I know
And the wider realms my eyes have never seen,
My mind is clear,
But my heart betrays a fear of what's ahead,
Where the grasses overgrow
And the wildness of nature shows instead,
Instead of ordered streets swept swiftly clean
With rows of storied buildings standing near.
Those silhouetted skylines spread
As early rays of dawn appear
And wake the living plains from sleep serene.
The change I undergo
Once every shade of dark has fled
Recalls how cities' corners overflow,
Encroaching toward savanna's gentle curving.
This threshold where my sight expands
Creates in me a conscience for conserving
What lands remain beyond our human hands.

Leaky Gutter

The drizzle outside was amplified
By a leaky gutter nearby.
Escaping drops drummed on the tops
Of iron roofs that lie
Just beyond my open window
As I stayed in bed, awake
But drifting in and out of dreams
That drew me, through a fool's mistake,
Forgetting they were less than real.
But consciousness was soon restored
By the truth that drummed on rusted steel
Where the leaky gutter's water poured,
Reminding me the rain was real.

Crescendo of the Rain

After midnight, I stepped outside
To gaze beyond my balcony,
And in the streetlights' glow I spied
The raindrops fall toward destiny.
I heard, below, a moment later,
The rising tide of their refrain.
Each bead performed as co-creator
In the bold crescendo of the rain.
One drop alone is something slight,
But when together, all their might
Can change the fabric of the night.

One walks along deserted streets
And in his eyes the water meets
To clear the tears that plague his sight
And join his lonely heart's continued beats.

Walking Through Rain

It was just a drizzle when I left
And had nearly ended when I arrived,
But in between, the clouds were cleft
In two, and every surface thrived,
Enlivened by the drumbeat of
The pouring rain from up above.
Puddles grew to a rippling pool,
While little rivers formed to rule
The roads where they were running.
Most people paused beneath a tree,
And they, perhaps, were far more cunning
Than I would prove myself to be,
My sneakers sopping wet despite
The little umbrella perched above my head.
I must have been a disheveled sight,
Pressing on through what the clouds had shed,
But as I reached my journey's end,
The rain was slowing up ahead,
And soon it stopped. The drops that did descend
Were dripping just from me.
Although I'd hoped to avoid rain's fall
While walking home, I find I'm free
Of anger toward the timing of it all.
I'm covered, drenched, but something's there
Within the molecules that share
Their bonds with me,
Supporting life across eternity.

Groundwater (Life Within the Earth)

Our water comes from underground.
We lift it up to great renown
With callused hands that pump and make it fly.

The tumbling of its rushing sound
Reverberates throughout our town
And brings relief when mouths are running dry.

But as our growing streets abound
With life, we threaten soon to drown
The well's capacity to get us by.

Our water comes from underground,
But every day we're drawing down
The level that remains of our supply.

No other sources have we found
Untainted by a dirty brown.
We must preserve what droplets lie
Pristine within the spaces underground.

Walking Past

I see you there but push on past.
I do not stop, though you have asked
For help from me, while I have cast
My eyes a different way.

Do I think your presence disappears
When my gaze diverts and I close my ears?
In truth, your pleadings pierce like spears
My heart with such dismay.

I wish the world were far more fair,
Where no one would be forced to stare
With searching eyes for alms to spare
When life has gone astray.

But as I ponder prayers for changes vast,
What help does this display
To the one I'm walking past?

Strange Thoughts

Somewhere
Out there
Is a stranger yet unknown to you.
Her care
You share
To preserve traditions strong and true,
But the songs hers strum
Are somewhat different from
The ones you've known and heard your whole life through.
Yet the beats upon her drum
From the streets her feet have walked have come
To present another, also valid view.
So, consider,
If you meet her,
That her thoughts, which seem to you askew,
Can offer something worth enshrining, too.

Baser Instincts

I don't know
Why you go
Always to a time
Few would try
To deny
Of another paradigm.
We've come so far since then,
But you remind me it was when
So much of how we live today
Began. A lion's den
Is safer than the words you say.
Advances which we overlay
Cannot create a new foundation.
A bit of quiet desperation
Can place our baser instincts on display.

Opening Moves

Some like to start offensively
And send their soldiers in
To break the lines aggressively
And sacrifice themselves to win,
While others wait, contentedly,
To build a strong position.
Both ways, they say, are possible,
So make your opening decision.
For me, I find preferable
The latter, though, admittedly,
The former holds its own appeal
To flame toward fortune instantly.
But I will turn a slower wheel
And flow, like water, patiently,
Until the time seems right
Perhaps to press for peace without a fight.

Bishops

The only pieces who only see
Half of the entire board,
And only when they both are free
Can every tile be, by them, explored.

The light, the dark – each has its squares,
And sometimes one is more involved
As kings conduct their grand affairs
In turns, until the conflict stands resolved.

Although the bishops seem unique
Among the pieces in the game,
They might be most like us, who peek
At glimpses of the whole, with none the same.

Only when combined, our stories
Illuminate this world's greater glories.

Knights

They leap from light to dark, and back to light,
Unhindered by the walls that block their way.
Their movements seem to go askew and stray
From other pieces' patterns. Every knight
Maneuvers round the structures of the game
With incremental progress, left, then right,
Until it finds a place to ease the plight
Of all whose movements fail to fit the frame
Defined by what is typical for most.
Its skilled maneuvers push aside the shame
And show its quality, of course the same
As others on the board. And so, the host
Accepts the ones they'd shunned until today,
But none should need to prove such worth to play.

Wheeling

Round and round your gliding goes
In the slanting light of the afternoon.
Above the roads' right-angled rows
You fly with wings outstretched, in tune
With every current of flowing air
To spin in spirals drawn with care.
What unseen tether leads you on,
Wheeling round and round, until
A few light flaps mean you are gone
To find some other space to fill
With feathered grace where the weather's fair,
To write your course which angels share?

A Bird Outside the Office

A bird outside the office
Was tapping on the window glass.
I whistled, and she cocked her head
As if in protest of that crass
And unrefined endeavor
To signal I would like to know
Her better.
Still, she sang, her eyes aglow,
Then fluttered off the ledge to go
About her day, with me behind.
I wish I knew what words she said,
For something in my heart has realigned.

Falcon Flying High

Falcon flying high
On a backdrop of sapphire sky,
What do you spy
Of the world here below?
What catches your eye
In row upon row
Of engineered surfaces
Static of flow,
With ill-defined purposes?
Forests used to grow,
Here banyan, there birch,
And each you could know
When gliding in search
Of a perch
To consider
The world here below.

The Dark but Starlit Heavens

I find myself upon a seat
That flies above the spinning sea
At thirty thousand feet,
A little world, enclosed but free
From all the surface conflict stirring
Beneath what I can see,
The broken lines between us blurring
As we together brush the sky,
Our common hopes enduring
To land once more where shores are dry
With safety and stability,
But still the ground will cry
For greater hymns of harmony.
Might we prefigure what we need
When in the clouds' tranquility
We set aside our greed
To glimpse the dark but starlit heavens
That shine on one humanity?

Uneven Ground

Walking on uneven ground
Acquaints me with the size and shape
Of every weathered mound
And all the grassy spots, which drape
The hillsides in their solitude
Whereon my footsteps scrape.
Tripping through what rocks protrude
Reminds me that our lives go round
In cycles fraught with pitfalls
Wherein our truest selves are found.

Where I Stand

How grand
To be aware
Of where
We stand,
The history
Of local land,
The memory
We share
Collectively
With every grain
Of sand
And gram of rain.
Instinctively
We know what pain
And joy and care
Expand
From what we see.
Serenity –
Does it impair
The purity
Of life's demand
To understand
The bare
Uncovered me,
And where
I stand
Within this fair
Ecology?

Married to the Meadow

You might suspect a word has been mistaken
In the title just above these first few lines,
But nay, the "to" will stay to reawaken
A partnership forgotten by our shrines
Of carpet-covered concrete, once constructed
To remind us of humility and care,
But sometimes now we cease to bow, instructed
To take control of anything we dare.
The meadow lives and is a true companion
For anyone who takes the time to see
Across what seems an interspecies canyon
But truly represents a single tree.
So, I must live in harmony, aware
That every limb deserves equality.

Elusive

Searching
Fingers exploring
Each steel string's tonality,
Searching for a melody
To hold,
Much like my living.
Each chapter's new modality
Seeks to make a memory
To hold.
Trying notes in simple combinations
And complex chords, whose subtle perturbations
Suggest a new tangential course
To hold,
Sends me off in undefined directions
Where wait as yet unknown connections,
But strains the grip on prior source
To hold.
Searching
Through it all, enduring
Every shift and change in harmony,
With hope to find some symphony
To hold,
Some true progression that links it all
And fits a purpose to every fall,
Persisting through each change in key
To hold.
What themes emerge from lives chaotic?
What meaning, more than mere quixotic
Struggles meant to mold a destiny,
Arises for each searching plea
To hold?

As It Is in Heaven

"Thy kingdom come," we pray.
"Thy will be done," we say,
On Earth, where all the shadows are,
Awash within their varied shades of gray.

For daily bread, we bleed
And barter every seed
We might have tried to plant someday,
But each is swallowed up by someone's greed.

Each trespass we commit
Or good deed we omit
Is met with malcontentment freed
By unforgiving eyes devoid of wit.

We struggle to define
What constitutes the line
Where justice and compassion sit
On separate sides, like water pure or brine.

Temptations lead us to
The ways we always knew
But can't escape, through some design
Delivered by the evils we accrue.

Yet still we pray, with hope
That someday, as we grasp and grope
For goodness on this Earth so far askew,
A whit of heaven's way
May redirect what's gone astray.
It's here, but needs uncovering anew.

For Thine

We add them on,
Almost as an afterthought,
A few final phrases
Flowing forward to the tune our parents taught,
But those whispered words
Are far from innocuous.
They speak still directly of
The greatest trials left to us.
We'd just jumped in thinking from
Forgiveness to temptation,
Then uttered of deliverance
From evil's devastation.
And now, we add them on,
Suggesting where the sweetest tempters lie:
The pull of power, the gain of glory,
The creeping call of kingdoms claimed on high.
"For thine," we say, are they,
And wise we are if we remember,
But often do we stray,
Desiring flames from every ember
Of influence and sway,
To carve our names forevermore
On tablets telling tales of time,
But even these are fleeting.
They crumble as new ages cross and climb
Through dynasties and destinies
And leave behind true memories
Of what we once had done with all our power.
So now, we add them on,
Those words reminding us that every flower
Must wither when its day is done,
But it will fertilize the soil
For those who next may blossom in the sun.
And Thou remain to tend their toil
Forever, through each hour eternal spun.

PART 2

AND LOSS

Final Moments

What happens in the final moments
As life's last breath is leaving?
Is the steady flow of time undone,
Unraveling before the cleaving
Of endless soul from mortal body?
What threads, remembered, run
Across the unencumbered sight
Of former days your footsteps spun?
And what of future stories held
Behind the curtain where we write
The actions of the present day –
Do they somehow come to light?
Do you spin within this web of moments
As past and future melt away,
With all in present tense occurring
At a point in time where you can stay?
Or will you softly slip below
While speeding with the light, inferring
How the world will change and grow
Beyond your days enduring?

Far Over the Weathered Mountaintops

Far over the weathered mountaintops
That rise above the leaves of shrouded trees
Enshrined in shadow after dusk,
An orange glowing fades to blue and black,
And evening's kiss of cooling breeze
Restores to you the freedom that you lack.

Far over the weathered mountaintops
Where you had roamed so many years ago
Along a still untraveled track,
You find yourself anew upon the brink
Of summits unexplored. Now go
And find the living waters there to drink.

Far over the weathered mountaintops
You fly, beyond the window by your bed,
While the remnants of your body sink,
And all of that confusion in your head
Disperses in a moment's wink.
Your spirit's on the wind, new trails to tread.

A Ship Went Sailing

A ship went sailing,
Sailing on the wind
Above the whispering waves and shivering oceans,
And it was scaling,
Scaling clouds now thinned
That veiled the distant stars' celestial motions.
Tonight, the curtain's failing,
Failing to obscure the whole
Whereon the wandering ship is traveling high.
Tonight, our love is trailing,
Trailing after every soul
Remembered like the starlight in the sky,
Whose memories are sailing, sailing,
Sailing back to brush a waiting eye.

The Undiscovered Island

There is an island
Forever just beyond horizon's ledge
Where all that's violent
Surrenders to the peace at water's edge,
And when you pass away
You'll walk the bridge that leads you to its shores
Though no one here can say
What dreams and futures wait within its stores,
But when I listen to the sparkling sea,
Sweet symphonies of you will come to me.

The Dreams Beyond the Dunes

To cross the threshold of the dunes
With straw-green grasses waving in the wind
And glimpse the crystal crests on blue-green gray
Advancing far until the tides rescind,
Each layer breaking over layer
And tumbling toward the steady shore,
Rumbling then releasing all its spray
As it splays across the sandy floor,
Reveals a mirror for the lives
That come and go, yet linger on
To soak into the souls of those
Remaining on the dunes when they have gone.
And one who stays is wondering
Where waves will wander after they have passed
That far off, strange, unknown horizon.
What currents come? What dreams will last
To reach the ancient shores of Avalon,
Where what was once, one day may be again,
And all transform to queens and kings
Whose lives of love will be remembered then.

All Our Yesterdays

Life is oft spent waiting
For what tomorrow brings,
But when it comes with sorrow,
When all your life no longer springs
Or runs throughout the hallways,
When one more time your head will lie
Upon the safe, unmoving ground,
When every sleepy stretch and silent sigh
Has ceased to spawn your searching gaze,
I yearn for all our yesterdays
And wish to hold you one last time,
Before your spirit must rebound
To where a better peace is found.
But each today that grace has given
Will live with me my whole life through.
I'll stand beside a windowsill
And find the breeze that called to you.

Residual Presence

Today, time took your soul away,
While I am left to wonder where you've gone.
Do paths exist where spirits stray,
Where you may listen, wait, and linger on?
I muddle through the world without you,
Wishing for the guidance of your hand,
But sometimes when I think about you
I almost feel as if you understand,
As if you know the thoughts I mutter
And watch the steps I take beneath the sky.
I hear the flower petals flutter
And wonder if your presence just passed by,
Yet you would likely wish for me to see
The beauty blooming right in front of me.

April in Her Eyes

I sometimes wonder where
Her little boy has gone
Who used to sit atop a wooden chair
Outside her house, upon a well-mown lawn.
But in my heart, I know
What sadness lingers there,
And trembling in the first December snow
Is grass that's overgrown in disrepair.
I sometimes glimpse her pacing
On garden paths when clouds are low.
It seems as if she's searching, chasing
Petals fallen months ago.
To drift beyond her hidden pains,
She lifts her gaze to breaking skies,
But always with the gentle rains
Of April in her eyes.

A Shadow in the Summer Night

Summer nights
When the lights go out
And the moss is bright with moonbeams,
Stars take flight
And the children shout
As they play amid their moon dreams.
The porch swing sways,
And someone prays
For safety in the coming storm.
The sky looks clear,
But something near
Suggests a cloud is taking form.
The kids come in
As the windows shut
In the face of what's amassing.
Chilled, her skin
Becomes chapped and cut
By a wind, like winter, passing.
Sweet summer nights
When the shadow bites
With the bitter taste of past despair,
A single strand
Of string will land,
Fallen from her gold but graying hair.
Her mind has gone
To remembered days
Spent within his loving presence.
But he's passed on,
And her dimming gaze
Searches far to find his essence.
The children come,
And her heartbeat's drum
Unravels as the moonlight glows.
The cloud has passed,
But its shadows last
As her string comes to rest where the moss still grows.

Autumn's Lullabies

Dark eyes press against the glass.
What do they see in the moonlight,
In the silver stars that touch the grass?
The shadows of September loom,
When the hours of night the day surpass,
A prelude to October's country
Where spirits gather beyond their doom
And dance their macabre scene.
Mountains rise, black-green
Against the backdrop of the night,
A phosphorescent glow beneath the moonlight,
But all the frights
Of devil, demon, wraith, and wight
Diminish before the morning
As stars, like angels, cast their lights
And break the latent bonds between
The visions and the eyes.
Chaos dissolves in falling leaves
Of laughter and autumn's lullabies,
And the little one who grieves
In early, long November sleeves
Knows, soon enough, true life again will rise.

Of Friendships Left Unfinished

What of friendships left unfinished
By the paths your life has chosen?
What of bonds that time's diminished
And the warmth that's since been frozen?
Do they wait for your remembrance
To return at once your call?
Or, do they disregard your semblance
After such a lengthy lull?
Or, perhaps you've somehow kept them all
Maintained since their beginning,
Preventing any gear to fall
Away from its continued spinning.
But some are not so fortunate
Or let their loving atrophy.
I fear a few of those I've met
Would find that circumstance with me.
Respectfully, I'd be obliged,
When someday I reach out to you,
If you'd forgive my faltered stride.
I'll try forgiving others, too.

What's Left When Letting Go

What right have I to brush aside your smiling
And share with you the tragedy that's fallen?
Your twinkling eyes, to me, are too beguiling,
And I wish not to make your morning sullen.

My body, lying still upon the landing,
Is waiting for your coming to be found.
I try to slow your steps, but as I'm standing,
You pass right through my spirit, now unbound.

The rain is falling, wave on wave unending.
Your eyes have cried the tears your sorrow needed,
Yet still I stay beside you, bent on mending
Whatever joy this passing has impeded.

What's lost is gone, and I must soon depart,
But I'd let go what's left of me
If it could heal your broken heart.

Tears on Pavement

You are crying –
I wonder if they're happy tears or sad.
No need for your replying
To tell me why today is good or bad.
Either way,
Those tears are flying
To splash upon the pavement wet and clear.
The droplets hold your story, drying.
Beneath the sun, they seem to disappear.
Yet through this change, evaporating,
They lift your hopes and fears beyond the sky.
The universe will hear, but I am waiting
To be with you regardless while you cry.

Deeper Down, a Distant Hue

What am I to do
When you
Are falling,
Falling down through shades of blue
Too deep to hear my calling?
Deeper down, a distant hue
Of darkness waits, deceiving
Those who think their virtues few
And life not worth receiving.
I wish you knew
It's all untrue,
And life's far more than grieving.
For now, I'll do what I can do
To keep your soul from leaving.
I'll wait with you
And keep your silent eyes in view
Until I see them glisten,
And every tear will be my cue,
Quietly, to listen.

For Better Worlds

What happened in the steps of someone's life
Who started as a wide-eyed child of hope
But has become a narrow-minded trope
Too jaded to believe the world can change,
Too skeptical of answers to the strife?
You started life with big ideas, strange
To huge, persistent structures at the core
Of what society suggests is more
Important – greatness, power, fame, and wealth.
You raged against the system's stifling range
Of tools to squelch your goals of moral health.
And now, you may resign yourself to be
A part of all this inhumanity
Or harbor endless anger in your skin.
You may perhaps be hoping, through some stealth,
To blow apart the structures from within.
Did living beat you down with every bend
Away from justice? Do you comprehend
The paths to power compromising each
Who throws a stone but stands not without sin?
We play the game but all our tricks of speech
Collapse beneath the weight of one small cry
Of one forgotten soul who sees the lie.
Remembrance of that innocent ideal
Restores your openness to those who reach
For better worlds – but can we make them real?

Stagnant

The faucet had been freely flowing
Much like a steady river running,
But then the drain had started slowing,
Surprising all our careless cunning.

Eventually, we turned it off
Or, at least, reduced the rate
At which the water filled the trough,
And now we're left to ask, "Too late?"

A tepid pool now lingers, waiting
Until the flow will start again,
While we remain at odds, debating
The right way to restart and when.

But as the present seems to stretch
And sit from day to day unaltered,
Perhaps we have the space to etch
A better future where we've faltered.

When future's bells return to ringing,
Perhaps the flow will pull us to
Release what vestiges were clinging,
Revealing light still shining through.

Spun Askew

When lovers wandered hand in hand
And children raced from door to door,
When every hour's falling sand
Revealed to us an altered shore,
Each moment of the world felt new,
But time has now been spun askew.
Although the planet's spin persists,
Our days are draped with stagnant mists
That swallow up our lives' progression
As we endure this plague's oppression.
We need a modicum of hope
To focus the uncertain scope
Of future's course, to give direction
And help us feel time's onward force –
A pathway toward renewed connection
To realign us with our source.

Pages Dispersed in the Wind

History flows,
Comes and then goes,
Pages dispersed in the wind,
Fluttering, flimsy, ascending the sky,
The writing exposed to the sun's blazing eye
And fading as morning clouds thinned.

Diaries close,
Thinking one knows
Destiny's every reply.
Sketchbooks keep capturing life's present trial,
But rainwater runs over memories while
The ink's not had time yet to dry.

Somebody sows
Seeds where what grows
Soaks up what falls from the sky,
And someone has saved a page from the wind,
A guide, enshrined on the wall where it's pinned,
To roots we forget and deny.

Their Daily Dance

She races in the morning, shining
While he is sleeping down below,
Yet in his dreams he sees her climbing,
Granting all her golden glow.
When noonday bells commence their chiming,
Her dance is dazzling every eye,
Yet with the evening's cold entwining,
Tiring, she'll go.

But that is when his face is growing,
Searching through the shadowed sky
Below the stars, above the foaming
Waves where strange reflections lie.
Each day and night, he goes on roaming,
Following her constant way.
At times, he'll catch her eye, which, knowing,
Sends its bright reply.

Round and round their forms are flying.
Rarely do their courses sway
To let them meet, for this aligning
Lays a shroud of deeper gray
Upon the day. So they, resigning,
Knowing that to stop would slow
Life's growth, resume their dance, denying
Where they pined to stay.

A Simple Thought's Enough

Why are we sad
When a simple thought enters the mind,
A simple thought that renders us blind
To the blessings around us we've always had,
A simple thought entwined
With a fear of what we'd lose
In the future's hidden folds and hues?
Why is our happiness undermined
By nothing more than baseless cues
Of what could follow down the line?
It grows like cancer. It sticks like pine,
But whatever the fates might choose,
Today, together, our faces shine.
That thought's enough, before the rest ensues.

Someday

Someday,
Your eyes will find me waiting
Within the hollow of a tree.
We forest nymphs go skating
Upon the frozen pond with glee,
But humans do not see.
When winter snow is falling,
We gather up the flakes to be
Our jewels, until the calling
Of springtime melts their essence free
To feed the forest's destiny
To come to life again and play.

Someday,
Your ears, anticipating
Our magic meeting, will agree
They heard a song creating
The blooming flowers on the tree
Where I will soon be waiting.
As summer's joys are flowing
For us who race the sunlight's beams,
I spy your sadness growing
For those who've left you, save in dreams.
The human heart's more knowing
Of life forever passed away.

Someday,
As autumn's rains are driving,
You'll find me in that hollow tree
Awaiting your arriving,
And on that day you'll see.
My eyes have watched you wishing
For magic to remove what grieves
Your days alone spent fishing
Where two before sat on the leaves,
But I can't wash your pain away.
Its permanence is strange to me.

Each year, the forest's leaves decay,
But they return, though differently.
Still, I will be your friend today.
We'll catch the falling tears that stray
From off your eyes, delaying,
To water life anew, someday.

Your Line Across my Heart

There are lines that run across my heart
And lead to those removed from me
By distance, sadness, strife, or time.
Each line is glazed in memory.

I wish to pull them all together,
But that would only pull apart
This web in which our lives are strung
Before new harmonies could start.

With every hour's steady chime
I touch the warmth in every tether,
The bonds to which my heart has clung
While shivering in stormy weather.

Do you, so far removed from me,
Detect, within the melody
I strum, your string sublime?

Water Without and Within
Psalm 22:14 – "I am poured out like water…"

If I cup my hand to catch the water falling,
A little pond appears upon my palm.
If I listen closely, I can hear the calling
Of words within the verses of a psalm.

I can't recall exactly how it goes,
But I know it has to do with water pouring,
Pouring out a king's imperfect soul
As he reflects on all his life's exploring.

As I hold the water waiting on my hand,
I wonder if he truly was forsaken,
Or if a spring could blossom in the sand,
Replenishing what many trials had taken.

I hear within my hand his far-off plea
So clear, for it exists as well in me.

Loose Threads

I know the way this story goes.
I've seen its fabric stitched like this before.
Unbroken seamlines juxtapose
The heroes and their foes arrayed for war.
But looking further toward the fringes,
I follow fraying edges unconnected
To all the knots on which this conflict hinges,
But still, the fight infringes
On where the loose threads lie, all unprotected.

Frayed

They said the act gets easier
The second time it's done,
And every instance following
With lesser friction would he run
His knife along the string
That holds a life stretched out from birth
Before he slices, quick and clean,
And severs it from Earth.

Although the task comes easier
With every rising sun,
The light he sees is darkening.
The thread he carries comes unspun,
For what his soul's been sanctioning
Is fraying every fiber wrapped
Within. Whose hand will intervene
To sever him from the role in which he's trapped?

Passed Pawn

The way ahead is clear
With none to block your path now drawing near.
You've risked it all to close
The distance to the goal behind your foes.
Success will bring promotion
And greater strength to match your pure devotion
To serve your gallant king
And fight a battle fit for bards to sing.

But you must also know
That, win or lose, the end will bring you low,
Returning to the role
You played before the battle took its toll.
And in your next campaign,
What changes, save your own traumatic strain?
The board remains the same
As kings send pawns to prosecute their game.

A King Came from Across the Sea

A king came from across the sea
And climbed upon my balcony
To catalog new lands to rule.
What mysteries he spoke to me
Of lives lightened by larders full
Of fragrant foods and waters cool,
Which conquered days of scarcity,
But something struck my soul as cruel.
His gaze grew as he turned to see
The bounty born of every tree
Beside the borders where I stay.
He thought this land his destiny.
His flag flew, ever on display
As what he saw was borne away
To fill his people's revelry,
But here he brought naught but decay.
A king came from across the sea
And swallowed up my history.
If I'd been born the same as he,
Would I have wrought such thievery?

Mountain Throne

He put a chair upon a mountaintop
And sat where none could reach him
Save for a pair of hawks whose flight paths drop,
Alighting there to teach him.
Theirs is a sight that spots each blade of grass
On plains so far below them.
But as the light of morning sunbeams pass,
He strains, unfit to know them.
Nothing his eyes will touch will look as sharp
As what the hawks would see.
Not built to fly where Apollo strums his harp
Is he. His melody
Lies in the bosom of this little Earth
Where we see somewhat clearly.
Within its passageways, we plant our worth
And hope it grows, sincerely.
Still, there are those who solely strive to climb,
To stand above, apart, alone,
But even mountains crumble, lost to time,
And so it goes with every throne.

Building Babel

Waking to the clangs of hammers
Hitting metal,
Making something rise above the trees,
Trucks deposit stones, which settle,
Slowly taken up
Amid the breeze
Blowing here ten stories high,
Hindering the progress toward the sky,
Scraping, grating, banging sound,
Sundering our speech upon the ground.
Groups divide as understanding wanes
While every speaker stammers,
Stuck beneath the swing of rumbling cranes.
Cracks create new dialects in space
Split up by concrete walls of class, whose grammars
Give no ground to grace an interface.

Giant

He strides upon the Earth
As if its every speck were his
To hold, to specify a worth,
And build what his desire is.
Each steps eats up a mile.
He wades across the ocean wide
And delves beneath the mountains, while
His passing makes all creatures hide
And hope for other days.
There was a time when he was small,
When greater herds could safely graze,
Before he stood so proud and tall.
With every footprint, forests fall.
Swung arms propel warm gusts of air
And whip up hurricanes for all
The mangroves on the coast. The glare
Of sun upon his eye
Reflects, refocuses, and burns
The valleys into deserts dry.
Transformed, the silent world turns
And wonders if his mind can learn
What consequences wait and rise
To make land boil and liquid churn
Before life's vanished cries.

In the Dragon's Aftermath

He stood upon a blackened field of rye.
The fire-breather's shadow loomed
Below the western sky.
He wondered if his life was doomed,
But looking toward the dragon's piercing eye,
He saw no note of malice there,
Unlike the drakes of old,
Whose greed was famed. Each caverned lair
Was lined with heaping piles of gems and gold
That glittered in the fiery glare
But left their master cold,
Then heroes of the stories rode
To best the beasts and win the world's renown,
Invading every dark abode,
Perhaps, to gain a crown.
Today, the tale has changed its mode.
The monster followed as a consequence
Of modern humans' hubris, bold
To manifest immense
Control of nature's every fold
And quench the magic of the wider world.
With this, the mighty dragon woke,
And, leather wings unfurled,
It rained destruction, burned and broke
The clockwork engines, gems of industry,
And brought the flames of which we spoke
With little urgency.
But now, the fires are burning low,
And standing there upon his field, he sees
A gentle rain to heal the woe
And wet the blackened trees.
It comes to fall on all alike
To quench this dragon of our own desire.
The beast departs, no more to strike,
Although it does not tire.
Its task is done, and all we'd built
Has crumbled into dust and come to naught.

He sees our great collective guilt
And every harm we've wrought.
He sees survivors kneel to pray,
Convicted by the dragon's long-told birth.
He sees new hope in what they say
Of future lives of worth,
Restoring what was lost today,
But now as humble stewards of the Earth.

Where Our Words Don't Rhyme

She woke this morning, gazed outside,
And fixed her eyes upon the elm
Our neighbor's grown with pride,
Within his little forest realm
Where filtered tales abide,

Tales of pretty preservation
Within a garden's sweet abode,
But all was devastation
Beyond where some few strains were stowed
Of nature's congregation.

We hoped those isolated bits
Would yet sustain what we've destroyed.
Now, desolation sits
Upon once fertile lands devoid
Of life which nature knits.

Those slight preserves don't hide our crime,
Our silencing of other song.
Perhaps it will return in time.
New forests grow through ages long
Composing where our words don't rhyme.

By the Light of a Broken Moon

Above your eyes, a crystal dome extended,
Enclosing and protecting you from harm.
We placed you here to keep your heart defended
From all the outer world's ugly charm,
For though your sight could penetrate the casing,
The image was distorted and made pure.
No matter which direction you were facing,
You viewed a landscape filled with nothing more
Than what we wanted you to see. But lately,
Despite your solitary nights and days,
You recognized the lie and knew, innately,
That something more was hidden from your gaze.
With all your might, your hands began their beating
Upon the glassy walls containing you,
And though you were afraid, you kept completing
Each strike to meet a world whose life rings true.
Then, suddenly, I saw my own deception
And found I'd let myself believe the lie
That if we shielded you from woe's reception,
You'd find a better life beneath the sky
That we had marred. I ran to you and shattered
The barriers between us. These were what
Had led to lives where all our souls were scattered,
Apart from one another, minds all shut.

Society had fractured into pieces,
Each fragment bent on gaining all it could,
Until the war that tore the final creases
Vestigial from when reaching out was good.
We scorched the lands to harden our division,
Acidified the seas, and built up walls,
But none of this could satisfy a vision
Of total separation. So, our falls
Were made complete when one competing faction
Gained power to exile others to the moon
And blast it into pieces. Now, one fraction
Or more is always seen, from night to noon.

You see our sins before you, far too many
To take in all at once beyond your dome.
You fall upon your knees, unsure of any
Response that could do justice to this home.
But then, you rise, embrace me, and forgive
The part I played to put you in seclusion.
The truth is cruel, but we will only live
By knowing every flaw without delusion.
What measure of redemption we might find
Begins with simple acts of understanding
To heal what wounds we can and keep in mind
The wrongs that left no more than remnants standing.

Purple Periwinkle Petals

Purple periwinkle petals
Upon the trees and scattered on the street
Adorn this space of fired bricks and reinforcing metals
With softness, scented sweet
Like honey on a summer's day.
Their influence is subtle and discreet,
When juxtaposed against constructed gray,
Yet still reveals our hardening conceit.
Purple periwinkle petals
Upon the trees and under striding feet
Perhaps will make us stop and think of how our progress meddles
With biomes once complete.

He Forgot the Forest

Born beneath a tree
But seeing brighter light beyond,
He stepped outside the branches' bond
To gaze on open sky.
Thus, he left the tree
As buildings in the distance beckoned.
All his bold ambition reckoned
That was where to fly.
But he thought he heard a faint reply:
"What do you see in the forest?"
Only the superseded lore
Of the past, nothing more.

Footprints from the tree
Had faded long ago, and now
He walks where city streets allow
Though they do not reply.
Faint, a memory
Of floors that give and breathe and answer
Below the touch of every dancer
Seeks to find his eye,
And he barely hears again that cry:
"What do you see in the forest?"
Something forgotten, never known
When walking the streets alone.

Now, no longer free
To walk wherever he wants to go,
Weighed down by age's undertow,
Confined to sit and lie
In bed, to always be
Alone, his drifting mind recalling
The drifting leaves, together falling
When comes their time to die.
Unheard, he speaks a final sigh:
"What do you see in the forest?
A life entwined with every tree,

Far better a home than only me."
At last, his spirit extends, to try.

And Now, the Rain

And now, the rain
Descends from roofs below a clear blue sky.
Inside each house is water solely found,
For elsewhere every drop has long been dry.
And now, the rain
Will never grace again the cracking ground
Beyond where shelters grow the only seeds
That germinate on shelves where they are bound.
And now, the rain
From condensation falls in little beads
That hang upon the ceilings made of glass
To satisfy the world's waning needs.
For now, the strain
Of all the years we let the warnings pass
Has broken through and burned once fertile earth
To leave behind decaying blades of grass.
Someday, the rain
May come from clouds again to bring rebirth.
Those left of us must listen to the flow
And show that we can know our greater worth
In humbler roles, sustainably to grow.

The Writings of the River

Over centuries, the river writes its story –
A tale of ebbs and flows,
Of gentle suns and storming throes
Of kingdoms and their glory.

Over dynasties, it carves a path –
Erosion, sediment, and time –
As periodic wars appear to rhyme
Though armies change and find new reasons for their wrath.

Over destinies, the river shifts its sands
Though each side claims the land was always cut
By one unchanging border, ever shut
Against another nation's greedy hands.

Over rhapsodies of battle and of mourning,
The river lifts its heavy song
And runs blood-red to purple seas as long
As present kings heed not its cold refrains of warning.

Over royalties, the waters rise.
The river swells to flood the thrones that stayed so dry.
The voices of the casualties refuse to die.
They wash away the kingdoms as they realize
They were all the same, despite each separate guise
Of flags and uniforms beneath the sky
And over mingled waters of the river,
Which writes of death and new rebirth, and tries
To guide the generations toward a different kind of prize.

Stand Before the Fall

Stand, stand beside the throne
Where kings build up their walls of stone.
Stand, stand and make it known,
A wider world is calling.
For we cannot exist alone
And separate from what life has grown
Beyond the realms we call our own,
Which ever more are sprawling.
Stand, as every sectioned land
Prefigures future's falling.

Moonflower

Each month, another bloom is born,
Beginning closed and dark,
But bit by bit, each night and morn,
All silver-white and stark,
It blossoms, filled with gossamer dreams
Of subtle light and spark
Reflected from the stars' bright streams,
Then petals fall and mark
The cycle of all life we know:
To grow and gleam, then, it would seem,
To wither, but in memory to glow.

PART 3

AND PEBBLES ON THE SHORELINE

Like Pebbles Cast Upon an Endless Shore

Each pebble cast upon the endless shore
Is etched with traces of the ancient tides.
Beneath its tiny surface shell is more
Than what is shown.
Each stone a deeper story hides.

Her Diary

Where will the pages take me today?
Far from the realm where I stand
Through histories, fantasies, fictions, and rhymes
With depths unknown on the sand,
A sliding kaleidoscope throwing the spray
Of magical oceans, where places and times
Cover the shores where the dreamers delay
And bask in those faraway climes.
The diary gingerly held in my hand,
Though only a memory, lives what she planned.

Ephemeral Bloom

Morning wakes, and with it comes a blooming.
A splash of color catches sun's first ray.
I, in its fragrant scent, delay,
For soon its petals' wilting fall is looming.
Tomorrow may its beauty pass away,
So I must write of it today.

Two Lines

Two lines run ever parallel, and though they never went askew,
I'm sorry I could never touch the hand outstretched from you.

Geometry

There's something pure about it.
No realm of space and shape exists without it,
And though its clockwork never falters,
At times, it seems, its surface alters,
Revealing new perspectives underneath.
And when we see its symmetry around us,
The shallow outlines given depth to ground us,
Each sword we've drawn will vanish in its sheath.

Pieces on the Board

You've placed me here,
Whether to capture or be captured, I'm not sure.
One thing is clear:
The loss will haunt both sides who wage this war.

When Walls Go Up

Brick on mortared brick, we build them up
With every absolutist proclamation,
Ignoring so much nuance in the overflowing cup
Of someone's heart and life's great conversation.
The more we see a world of walls and never-yielding stone,
The more our souls will find themselves alone.

Brought to Boil

The fire's lit, and heat is swelling
Along the borders of the pot,
Where tiny bubbles start their telling –
The water's getting hot.
Once peaceful, now the surface pops,
Explodes, its tension all expelling
Where too much sun has killed our crops
And we've been left to rot.

Undone

A cloud
Spun
Across
The sun
To shroud
The ground
We've won.
What loss
Is found
Where blood
Has run?
All nature
Comes
Undone.

Until the Night Is Over

Stay with me until the night is over,
Until the dawn's own dew anoints the clover
Where groves of trees had grown before.
We cut them down at dusk, and darkness shone.
It brought the longest night we've ever known.
Stay until trees live once more.

Sheets of Rain

Why does rain come down in sheets?
It's not a blanket warming those beneath,
Nor, I think, a page of written word,
But maybe one for music, which I've heard
In drizzle's calm and thunder's gnashing teeth.
Each droplet draws a note when ground it meets.

Stretching Toward the Rains

Someday when the rains
Come
We'll find new food again,
But until then,
We'll wait
And stretch what quantity remains,
Some
Each day to put upon a plate.

A Storm Before

Streams of water tumble down
From clouds that nearly touch the ground,
Appearing like a pale-gray gown
That shrouds the air, and rhythm's found
Within the rumble of the hail
Which pounds below, while thunder drums on high.
The storming slows. Light thins the veil.
Remaining droplets hanging from the rail
Are lenses toward a distant bright blue sky,
Prefiguring what peace will follow nigh.

When Cloudy Skies Are Broken

When cloudy skies are broken
And the sun shines through again,
What words of praise are spoken
For the light that warms us then,
But in the cracks of an arid plain
The clouds bring life, relief, and rain.

Fallen Flowers

Upon the sidewalk after rain
Are flowers, fallen from the strain
Imposed by stormy winds and water's weight.
The chimes of chance have changed their fate.
Where once the flowers blossomed bright,
They've come to occupy a mud-stained plight.
Aloof, our footsteps undermine
And crush the dreams their lives define.
Yet still, their colors grace the sidewalk's grain,
Downtrodden souls whose rays of hope remain.

Nighttime Breezes

A breath of air makes the open window's curtains flutter.
What whispered words do the nighttime breezes utter
As they pass inside
And fill what secret spaces hide
To softly sing me to sleep.
What whispered words reach my dreaming deep
Where their wisdom clears away the daily clutter?

Of Vines that Hang from Power Lines

They wind themselves around when they have found it.
Eventually their growing leaves surround it.
The power line supports them as they try
To stretch a little closer to the sky,
But when the power's cut, and night goes dark,
Their energy maintains its living spark.

Trimming of Hedges

Sometimes I wish there would be no trimming of hedges,
That we'd let them grow to engulf the concrete ledges
Where we walk or stand or sit and stay awake,
No space for dreaming dreams of what we'd make
If we let the world be what it will be
And conform ourselves to the contours it would take,
Rather than working the other way around
Where it's forced to fit our footprints on the ground.

Beneath the Overhanging Branches

The light of a summer Sunday afternoon
Is filtering through the leaves above my head,
And, though you would think the light must lesser be,
The branches contribute more where shadows spread.

Open Water Running

There's beauty in the simple sight
Of open water running.
Even in a drainage ditch
The rippling rivulets are stunning,
Sparkling in the midday light,
Weaving through the refuse, tumbling
Ever down the deeper ditch
Toward greater waters rumbling.

Stewardship

Pick some flowers, you may,
But you must not pick them all.
Some must in the meadow stay.
Can you hear tomorrow's children call?

Home

A home that stands without four walls,
Its ceiling blue and white, and black as night,
Its floor, here soft, there hard, which sprawls
Beyond the reaches of my farthest sight,

Its shining lights, from moon and sun,
Illuminate its new and ancient scars.
Our task: to mend what harm we've done,
Inflicted on our home beneath the stars.

Now in Harmony

Today is nothing less
Than any other day upon the Earth.
So why do I digress
From now, assigning to it lesser worth
Than days enmeshed in memory
Or futures built on nothing but projection?
I need to heed the harmony
That comes from every moment's introspection.

Closest to You

I find myself feeling closest to you
When the rhythm of rains blankets the grass,
When the sunshine warms where hummingbirds pass,
When through dimming of dusk gleams night's first star,
When the whistling of wind carries tales from afar,
When anything grants me the grace of a view
Toward more of the world that pours out from you.

Spring Dawn

Daylight plays upon the hills
Dancing to the sound of someone singing.
Early in the morning to displace the dark time's chills,
Dawn emerges like a fountain springing.

Roadside Gardens

I walk alone through shades of brown and gray
On streets and sidewalks paved with brick and stone,
But close at hand, I see more colors play
With green and gold and violet. Glad I am to stray
Wherever flowers, leaves, and trees have grown.

White Tails in the Sky

We stop to ask what planes fly by,
Writing lines across the bright blue sky.
Those tails of white give no reply,
So our eyes return to gazing nigh.

The Sounds of Warmth

Warmth is a feeling, they say,
But I hear its music at play
In the crackle of logs on a winter night's fire
Or the songs of the birds that spring morns inspire,
In the rolling of waves beside pale summer sand
Or the rustle of autumn leaves quilting the land,
And, most impactful of all to me,
In the voice of a friend from across the sea.

Warmth from Words Within

When the air is cold
And the wind comes rushing in,
The fire goes out
And the light is growing thin,
But the flame you hold within
Is ever bright.
It burns without
Extinguishing tonight.
Every tale you're told to write
Feels uninspired,
But the words that spring from you
Are more desired.

Fallen Leaves in Mountain Streams

The colors lining mountain streams
Are different when the air is cold,
When naked trees, asleep in winter dreams,
Allow their fallen leaves to fold
One upon another, gold
And red and brown, with violet seams,
To form a bed where rushing water gleams.

What Magic Lives in Christmas Lights

What magic lives in Christmas lights?
What wonders wait inside the stars
That touch our hearts on Christmas nights
And ease the year's most troubled scars?
It's something sprung from home, and friends,
And family – each meeting sends
Me onward with the grace to know
Of blessings, all reflected in
That multi-colored Christmas glow.

Shining Bright

When all is said and done,
When all we've been will be distilled,
What more could anyone
Desire than to be compared
To you, who in your living filled
The world with thoughtful, unimpaired,
And caring light –
Today, as ever, shining bright?

Sundown Symmetry

Sundown on a never-ending lake –
That ball of fire slips behind the water,
But what remains above remains awake
And mirrored in a world below the sky
Where liquid flames cast light back toward my eye.
The moment comes when half the sun has set –
The whole appears, as one's reflection's met.

A Final Glow of Gold

The sun has dropped beyond my sight,
And darkening blue-gray clouds traverse the sky,
But then a window opens in the west,
And the cloud face there, still touched by daylight's eye,
Reflects those rays to me, whose night is blessed
By a final glow of gold before I rest.

Lightly Do the Leaves Fall

Lightly do the leaves fall
Despite the heavy rain,
Which pounds upon the branches tall
And drowns the ground's domain.
The world is changing, draining all
Of what once was away,
But lightly do the leaves fall
To float on what new rivers run today.

Walking and Writing

Each step invokes the wonder all about,
And I can't help but search for words to write,
Imperfect as they are, and laced with doubt
That what my pen creates will come out trite,
But what alternative is left to me
When every step suggests a symphony?

PART 4

WHERE THEY CROSS

Let Them In

We try so hard
To push the magic out
And hide what hopes we feel with stoic covering.

We try to disregard
The wonder all about,
Forgetting life beyond the deadlines hovering.

We have our moments, rarely,
When stars align, unveiling
The strings that spread across the cosmos, glistening.

Perceptible, just barely,
Their sounds are never failing,
And we are free to let them in by listening.

Two Faces

Some pebbles have two faces
With one side rough and ragged,
The other smoothed with every jagged
Edge worn down by fortune's paces
Over time.
But still they climb
The tides as one
With two perspectives always spun
On everything the world brings,
Whether coal or diamond rings.
The two see different sides of spaces.
One looks above, the other under,
Yet both still see some wonder,
If only gleaned in traces.

Two Perspectives of a Roadside Hedge

Over the Hedge (Toward the Heavens)
Over the hedge
Beyond that wall of branch and leaf and green
Lies something more,
Something brighter than my eyes have ever seen.
For where I walked before
Was veiled in shade below its topmost edge
To guard my fate,
But now I hunger for
The hidden lore
And brilliant sheen
That wait
Just past the hedge.

A Hole in the Hedge (Toward the Earth)
There's a hole in the hedge,
Which I might crawl through
To explore other realms
And locations new,
Which were blocked before,
Reasons why unsure,
But the barrier broke,
Which expands my view.

Two Responses to Pleasant Dreams

Where Do Dreams Go (Obsession)
Where do dreams go
When waking brings an ending to their race?
Do lives endure and flow
Though they recede to some subconscious space
Within my head?
When I arise from bed,
Do those who graced my slumber cease to be,
Or might I find their presence in a place
Beyond the shores of fading memory?
If so, I'll wander high and low
And lose myself to bring you back to me.

Dreams of You (Appreciation)
Dreams that bridge the darkness bring me through.
In them, I'm blessed to see a smiling face
Whose beams of light the nighttime treats as true.
At break of day,
They fade away,
But I retain a whispered trace
Of you.

Whose Story

To go through life as if it were a story
With me the hero, gaining greater glory
At each expectant point along the way
Just waiting for my central plot to stray
Toward its realm,
To pit myself against all other foes
Who also look to be the one who goes
Along the hero's journey through a field
Of conflict to be tested with a shield,
Sword, and helm,
Suddenly feels wrong.
This story lingers far too long
For one so small as me
To fill its fullest destiny
Myself. Perhaps my goal
Should be a strong supporting role
To help some others find their trail
While drifting, peaceful, tale to tale,
And overall, contributing
To something more than I alone could sing.

In What Seems Small

I search for oceans vast and teeming
Or rivers running full and fast and wide.
What else could circumscribe your dreaming,
Which knows the time and course of every tide?

She stands, instead, beside a tree
And watches as the rain is lightly gleaming
Beneath the golden sunlight, free
From breaking clouds whose outer shells are steaming.

I wonder what her mind is thinking
To focus on so small a symphony.
What majesty could she be linking
With tiny beads of liquid mystery?

Then suddenly, I see it all
By following her eyes, whose gaze unblinking
Aligns with one about to fall,
One drop that holds the world before its sinking,

A lens delaying on a leaf
Before its contents splashes with the call
Of gravity, while I in disbelief
Find you reside still more in what seems small.

Until the Veil Is Lifted

Can you hear the grass grow?
Can you feel the stars glow
When the rhythm of the heart
Skips a beat, comes apart?
All the world seems to slow
While the scene, like painted art,
Draws the eye to row on row
Full of flowers, nature's start
In tracing what true beauty is.
Never being hers or his
Or anyone's to own,
Beauty's beads are gently blown
To all, and none can lay a claim.
Faces show themselves, alone.
Veils no longer hide the shame
Of pride in who we thought we were.
Spirits sting and angels stir,
And soon, among the silent stones,
A voice is heard as we endure
The truth deep-set within our bones
Of flaws and faults and thoughts impure,
But also, through unvarnished tones,
Of humbler selves, to build a cure.

The Winds of Change

It's indescribable,
Yet somehow undeniable
For me, as I reflect on where I've come
Through all the years and all the weary
Moments. Imperceptible
Has been the silent hum
Of choirs undeterrable
In days of sun or darkness cold and dreary.

Leaves rustle,
Branches bend,
And all the busy, excess bustle
Can fall away to point me toward a blend
Of what my life should always be
And how my soul is most complete.
The winds of change surrounding me
Have brought me back for us, again, to meet.

Beside the Sunset Bay

Calling softly, seagulls fly
Above my head to touch the sky.
Water in the bay recedes,
And all the children wonder why
Time uncovers waiting weeds
As low tide pulls the waves away.
Salted seafoam breezes play
Across the sand the sunshine feeds,
While the water's bluish gray
Complexion satisfies the needs
Present on a distant shore,
Where other children's visions soar
To spot the seagulls in the sky.
Still, this roaming troubadour
Will see the cycle, wet and dry,
Wishing to reflect upon
The storied patterns come and gone.
Where does every moment stray
When tides propel it past the dawn?
Perhaps it floats away
To rest beside a sunset bay.

Above the Stars of Eden

Above the stars of Eden burns
A night without an ending,
And, out of it, a presence turns
To gaze upon the life ascending
Upon a small, revolving world
Of blue, with green that's newly growing.
A consciousness has come uncurled,
Commenced its crawl to greater knowing,
But with its rise, the chance to fall
Comes too, and, with each new discerning,
The danger heightens. Life stands tall
To reach beyond its station, learning
That therein lies the path to progress
But also, possibly, its own undoing.
The cosmic presence watches all
And asks which way this garden's life is going.

The Sculptor and the Sculpture

"If I may,
I'd like to shape you out of clay,"
Said the sculptor to the sculpture
As his hands began to play.
The art was yet unrealized,
But the artist had devised
His plan to bring the thought to life –
Then, suddenly, he improvised.
He introduced an imperfection,
Removed a fairly central section,
Then covered up the hollowed hole
Invisible to eye's inspection.
Some magic in the sculptor's mind
Gave breath, and atoms realigned
To live, as all creation paused,
For here was something new defined.
It felt the air expand its chest.
At first it seemed content to rest,
But then it yearned for something more
And started on an endless quest.
Was it correct, this sculptor's ploy,
To make the sculpture search for joy
Outside itself? It's led to greed
And wars from Jericho to Troy.
But there are times in life's great trial
When what is lacking turns the dial
And spurs us toward a better world.
It's then we see the sculptor smile,
For, though it's difficult to fathom,
The sculptor named the sculpture Adam.

To Touch the Sky

What does it mean to touch the sky?
That bright blue ceiling strikes the eye,
But nothing's really there.
It's just the atmospheric air,
Which gently thins and dissipates
As I ascend through cloudy gates
And glimpse a solar flare.
Nothing solid – wall or snare –
Will stop my elevating climb
(Neglecting gravity, this time).
The nighttime sky is where
I see the true extent laid bare.
Infinities of dark amass
Above my head. There depths surpass
My sight beneath the glare
Of glassy stars. But don't despair
Or lose your dreams of touching sky.
Forever reaching, striving, try
Each time, again, with care,
To struggle further forward, where
New realms will dare your eye.

Drinking in the Moonlight

Willows blow and flowers grow
Beside the flowing waters of the river.
A subtle breeze through silver trees
Awakens leaves that rustle, shake, and quiver,
Whispering the wisdom of the night.
Willows know that flowers glow
When moonbeams throw their lights like phantom lances
Through branches where she steps with care
To not impair their courses as she dances,
Christening the dawning of the night.
Then when each willow's drunk its fill
And flower's beauty lingers,
She'll catch a moonbeam, hold it still,
And feel its magic through her shining fingers.
Then finally, her face full bright,
She'll swallow up her fleeting plunder
To feel the glow of a moonlit night
In this sparkling white wine of wonder.

The Night, Awake

The crescent moon, a pale and sleepy eye,
Extends its gaze across the blue-black sky,
As stars appear like tears upon a face
That knows not why it condescends to cry
When breezes bring, within its breath, a trace
Of growing life from fertile soil's grace
Where brown-black grains of graded silts and clays
Define the depths of land's creative space
As locusts hum above and moonlight strays
In filtered silver beads through wooded ways.
At times like these, when all the senses spy
The oneness of the world's songs and plays,
You feel your smallness shrink below the sky
Although its dreams of you exceed its eye.

Tunnel Through the Night

A gentle hum and sway
Accompanies the dreamer's way
On tracks that lead us on from dusk to dawn.
The passing scenes outside are drawn
With shades of black and bluish gray
And points of light that blur before they're gone.
The dreams and stories spun
Inside the gliding cars can run
Beside the sliding pictures in the glass.
Although the realms of thought surpass
Reality beneath the sun,
There's magic in each darkened blade of grass
That sparkles in my sight
And shapes the lives that tunnel through the night.

The Angel of the Sounds of Night

When all the sounds collect
Between my listening ears,
More wonderful than I expect
Are harmonies, and she appears,
Allaying all my fears.
Arrayed in rainbow light
That swallows up my stagnant tears,
She hovers in her dreamlike flight,
Inspiring me to write
The growing melody
That echoes through the mystic night
Behind the silence, setting free
A creativity
That rushes to the Earth.
All manner of what's heavenly
Arise to greet the new dawn's birth
And share their songs with me.

Light and Shadow

Even beneath the blazing midday sun
I still cast a shadow on the ground.
The dark extends from me, no matter where I run,
But without the light, the shade would not be found.

We want to dwell in the light
But avoid revealing the dark we try to trap,
And so we stand apart to escape the fright
Arising when our shadows overlap.

It's easier at night, when shadows hide
Beneath a charcoal sky where nothing's burning,
And buffers need not be so very wide
Between you and me, for eyes are less discerning.

But there's more to being close than seeing faults.
There's comfort too, for once our shadows share
A space to dance the circles of a waltz,
We accept each other, laying all our secrets bare.

And then, perhaps, we can stand beneath the sun,
To face the shadows it reveals as one.

To Melt and Freeze Again in Time

The climbing sun begins to melt the ice
That covers up the path I walk today.
The spreading liquid slides itself away
And wonders if this freedom has a price.

In time, it joins a cyclical array
Of vapor, cloud, and rain in warmer parts,
As stars look down on all the grateful hearts
Who thank the light for water as they pray.

In time, a new returning journey starts
To bring it back to its beginning place,
Refreezing in the falling night's embrace.
I stay and gain the wisdom it imparts:

In time, it will be gone without a trace,
Except for all the lives it touched
As it traversed this space.

New Days, Old Truths

We feel we've come so far
Throughout the past two thousand years,
So brief within the lifetime of a star.
We say we've fashioned shovels out of spears.
Our flags now fly on mountaintops
And lunar surfaces to spar
With cosmic rays, while earthly fields of crops
Feed billions through their days. And yet, we scar
Ourselves and all creation
With wounds akin to days before.
Men still seek power, wealth, and elevation
Above their peers, but push aside the poor.
We still pit one against the other
And fight our wars as if
We do not need the sister or the brother
Opposing us across the cratered cliff.

We still need ancient wisdom born
Of truths that hold from elder days.
The sun returns each newmade morn
To grant us all its warming rays.
We still need mercy laced with hope
In things unseen and thoughts unknown
To guide us toward a wider scope
Of love that forms a servant's throne.

White Wings in Search of Hope

White feathers cover wings that cross the sky,
Descend, and land upon a wooden perch.
Clear eyes watch through a window. People fly
To decorate their trees, wrap gifts, and search
For memories of Christmases gone by.

Another landing spot outside a church
Reveals the melodies of carols. High,
Imperfect voices, singing softly, lurch
From note to note, and wonder if their sound
Will touch a chord of greater harmony.

Beneath a twinkling streetlight, on the ground,
A man's unfocused eyes look up to see
A glint of hope within the stars, unbound
By hints of distant hymns, whose symphony
Is floating on a wind the wings had found.

As if in answer to a tacit plea,
The man begins to walk, his sight aligned.
He gathers up the memories that he
Has held inside, and hopes that he might find
What mercy holds for this long-absent one.

Clear eyes watch through a window. People dined
With thoughts bent on the past, but now they run
To meet it, knocking at their door, defined
By much regret. They welcome home their son.
White wings ascend this night of hope, now done.

Higher than the Clouds

Go higher than the clouds
That hover round the mountaintops,
Surpass the wispy shrouds
Before their waiting water drops
And see another mountain-scape
Whose fluffy summits billow up
Where unimpeded sunbeams drape
Themselves upon the slopes.
An open hole suggests a cup
For light to pour its shining hopes
That touch the ones below the clouds
Whose vision does not penetrate
The layerings of spreading shrouds,
To see the brighter things that wait
Beyond and in each shadowed head
Where hope springs new and angels tread.

Great and Small

(based on a line from Homer's Odyssey*)*

You "think yourself a great man
Because you live in a little world."
Better it is, I think,
To be a small man
In a wide world,
To see your gaze stretch far and sink
Inside the wonders in the depths of every night,
The magic in each word the poets write.
And even better yet, perhaps,
To be a right-sized man
In a right-sized world,
To find your place
And fill that sacred space
With great reserves of love, and then collapse
The borders of your heart until
Each little grain of living wraps
A world within itself, where atoms spill
Upon your soul
And make the wider world whole.

Where the Stillness Rests

When every sound is silence
And every vision dark,
When any move is violence
Against the soul's redeeming arc
Arising from its meditation,
The truth becomes the destination
That graces life with wisdom's spark.
"What truth?" I hear the stillness ask,
As if it hopes to soon embark
From where it rests to bask
In wisdom far removed from here,
And I feel rise a touch of fear,
For every word is incomplete,
Each spoken thing, at best, a piece
Of some unfathomed whole we meet
Where reason stops and stories cease.
Beyond the sounds our mouths can utter,
Eternal chords, far deeper, flutter
But vanish when we train our ear
And try to capture what they say
Or write them down to make them clear.
The fuller part remains astray
Unless we let the stillness rest
And know the truth's an endless quest.

Raindrop Journeys

The newly-christened liquid water falls
In tiny packets sliding from the storm,
And entering the forest's wooded halls,
They follow many paths of varied form
Eventually to reach absorbent soil
Where, percolating, they will feed the trees.
Some sink before the clouds have stopped their toil,
At once to join organic alchemies
Transmuting life from separate elements.
But other droplets take their time to drift
From upper canopies with ornaments
Of flower, fruit, and vine before they gift
The ground with what sustains this old-grown place
They travel, dripping down from leaf to leaf,
And crawling round the branches as they trace
Their paths that, in the sun, remain so brief,
Evaporating to ascend the air
And start again. The droplets run their race,
But reaching first to win is not their care,
For every moment's journey is a grace
Enlightened as the sunlight pierces through
To capture all the beauty in its space.
So, follow every branch and learn anew
How each unique direction adds to you.

A Sunset Captured in a Drop of Rain

The orange sphere is racing just ahead
Of dark-gray sheets that sweep across the sky,
Collecting shades of pink and purple-red
Where rays of light impart their sun-made dye.

The sphere appears to touch the distant ground
And flatten, as the sheets begin to pour
Their water from above, its muffled sound
Surrounding me upon the grassy floor.

One cloud-borne tear falls just before my face,
Descending on the course it's meant to fly,
And in that moment – that brief, eternal moment –
One droplet holds the sun before my eye.

The Sun Behind the Storm

Where does shelter lie
To offer solace from the storm?
Do you wall the endless sky
And close off every face and form
Until your soul is held inside
And nothing enters through the door?
But what of those who wait outside,
Enduring still, as times before,
The lashings of the driving rain,
The pressures of eternal strain?

No – today, I open up
To hear the cry and see the cup
Where dreams deferred spill out again
To break upon the ground, and then
I reexamine what I think
And learn from lives that bend their ink
To mark the struggles they have known,
Each loss and wound and broken bone,
And so much time spent waiting
For all to hear the devastating
Song that pours until reform
Will find the sun behind the storm.

For the sun is sometimes brightest
When it's breaking through the falling rain,
And the air is sometimes lightest
In the shadow of the hurricane.
Will the days soon bring that moment?
Will the swelling waves and fair refrain
Bring all humanity to bear,
Confronting such historic strain
With deeper strands of love? Ensnare
My humble soul, in days grown warm,
Where solace lies beyond the storm.

When Warmth Returns

Today, the sun's come closer in the sky
To burn away the breaking clouds that fly
And fade away to nothingness.
Unshaded leaves reply.

They drink in sunlight's unconstrained caress
To grow beyond the colder season's stress,
While I recall, as if anew,
What warmth the days express.

And far beyond the frame where lifetimes drew
Their journeys on a canvas spread by you,
I'm ready to begin again
And search for more that's true.

Your Worth Beneath the Sun

She walks the earth with head hung low,
Unsure of where she fits.
She's watched the skies and searched below
And seen the way the spirit splits
In two when someone makes a choice,
Resolving toward a certain chord.
Regretful phantoms lend their voice
To the road left unexplored.

But regardless of the path that's chosen,
You've made the choice your own.
I could say your burning doubts are frozen
By the branch of life you've grown.

What deeds you've done,
What songs you've sung.
Do you know your worth beneath the sun
Ever since the air first rushed to fill each lung?

But beyond an account of acts alone,
A more fundamental undertone
Recalls to mind a lullaby
For babies, birds, and bards who've yet to fly.

Even if you didn't do
The amazing things you've done,
Your endless value still stands true,
For you live within life's web beneath the sun.

So lift your head and hold it high.
Your worth would more than fill the sprawling sky.

Speak Your Story Soon

Speak your story soon
By the light of this expectant moon
That lingers on horizon's line for you,
A tale of someone's tune
That sounded on a sand-swept dune
But languished as time's whistling breezes blew.
She called for him to listen
When the wave crests tumble, break, and glisten,
To hear the world's wonder whipping through.
At first, he felt it beckon,
But in time, his trembling mind would reckon
That wisdom waits in other places too.
Although he'd not been wrong,
He'd lost the tune of her moonlit song,
Which glimpsed a hint of the root of all that's true.
His journeys brought him far,
But the quiet strumming of a street guitar
One evening on a stone-paved avenue
Reminded him once more
Of the verses shared upon that shore
And the chords of something greater beyond his view.
Her voice was always calling,
Forever sending love and sprawling
Across the waves from which she takes her cue.
On distant winds, he heard
The echoes of her affirming word,
And it pulled him back to the place from which he flew.
So, speak your story soon
For I've returned with the rising moon
To listen and to humbly learn from you.

Words of Life

Pens write on pages torn
From Gideon Bibles in hotel drawers.
Printed type is covered; born
Are freer curves, like fertile spores
That blow across the nighttime air.
Ancient prose and poems past
Provide foundations, concrete cast
For architectures bold and bare.
Fragmentary thoughts are drawn
In words and sketches on each leaf
Until, as with a fresh-cut lawn,
The scent of life refines belief.
Human struggles, failings, flaws
Collect within the flowing ink
And mirror what the prophets think
Of ancient kings and lands and laws.
Past and present join as one
To share the promise and the pain
When every plan has come undone
And unintended scars remain.
Offer up what words will come
From liturgy and light
Of present days, whatever's right,
And God will build a greater sum.
Somewhere, by a desk lamp, bright
With blessings born of darkest night,
One finds afresh the perfect grace
That grants imperfect faith a place.

When Angels Dream

When angels dream
Beside the calm of heaven's stream
Within a golden forest glade
Where branches overlap and braid
The silver starlight's gleam,
What sights enshrine your haloed heads
And blossom in ambrosial beds
Of purely known unconsciousness?
What dreams arise when all is less
Than where you lie?
My dreams are less than yours, I think,
For my imperfect thoughts will shrink
And shrivel, fallen leaves that dry
Beneath a swollen sunlit sky.
But when your thoughts are close at hand,
My own proceed to fly and stand
Like trees that drink from deeper stores.
The golden forest stream explores
The higher realms that angels share.
With you as guide, I'm nearer there.
And so, I ask, so selfishly,
If once, tonight, you'll dream of me.

Upon the Rings of Saturn

Upon the rings of Saturn,
A never-ending highway runs
Whose every curving pattern
Holds stardust from a million suns,
And gazing at its pure designs
Beyond the scale of earthly craft,
Her understanding realigns
To offer up a final draft
Of something she's been wondering
Since starlight struck her infant eyes:
For all life's throbbing thundering,
Its laughter and enraptured cries,
So much is silent, by design
Or some gigantic happenstance.
The universe is still, a shrine
Where sterile planets spin and dance,
Unless there's more beyond her sight
Far further out in deeper space
Or underneath the day and night
That cycle right before her face.
She does not know, but she believes
That as she gazes at the rings
Of Saturn, something new achieves
Fulfillment, touching all good things.

Spiral Ascending

Somebody's knocking
On the door I'm unlocking
As rain droplets drum overhead.
Who could be standing
On the edge of my landing
To wake me so early from bed?
The door opens wide,
And the stairwell is dyed
With a shadow of somebody waiting,
But that presence moved on,
Ever higher it's gone
Toward the clouds and the storms they're creating.
I follow its track
Never once looking back
Up the steps in a spiral ascending.
Upon reaching the top
On the roof, I stop,
Anointed by raindrops descending.
But no one is here,
Though I thought it was clear
That someone before me was leading.
I feel something around me.
Its essence confounds me,
Then it dissipates, slowly receding
Unknown and unseen as the storms disappear.
With the dawn comes the calm I've been needing.

When the Circle Saw the Sphere

The circle lived its life within a plane
Aware of width and length, but not of height,
Yet finally, when granted greater sight,
It soon perceived what it could not explain
Before:
A sense of more
Beyond dimensions where its surface grew
And slid amid the other shapes. One tier
Within a many-layered chandelier
Was all it was. So much else was true.
The circle's friends were greater than they knew
Inside their plane perspective. They endure
As cylinders and prisms, cubes and more
That fill the space above, below, and through,
And finally, this newfound sight made clear
The circle is itself a full-formed sphere.

To Grasp at Higher Things

We stand upon the Earth
But search the sky to catch a star.
We sit upon the grass
But stretch out toward horizons far
Beyond familiar fields of birth
From which our story springs.
Through unexplored terrain we pass
To grasp at higher things.

At least, that's what we tell ourselves
As we travel wide and deep
Through air and sea and space
And stranger dreams in realms of sleep.
But far beyond where each step delves
The universe observes our flaws
And knows we're nothing but a trace
Of matter made by nature's laws.

At least, that's what our eyes believe
As we stretch to touch night's starry strings,
But hidden depths our hearts perceive
And gasp, as choirs sing.

To Wake Anew the Future's Dreams

Call me back from where I roam
In dreams whose trails of shifting loam
Confound my course and cause my soul to stray.
I wander far through mist and foam
In memories once molded out of clay,
Now nothing more than reveries
With still familiar melodies,
And though I might desire to stop and stay,
I must move past their welcome breeze
To wake anew the future's dreams today.

Little Miracles

It seems they used to come much bigger,
Much bolder, brighter, more apt to trigger
A sense of unencumbered awe
Toward what the prophets said they saw.
The dead arise.
The sick are well.
The bread in baskets multiplies.
A word makes storming quell.
Beyond the wonders stories tell,
They still appear in altered guise.
Within each moment, something lies
That leaves me struck beneath its spell:
The sunlight touching flower blooms,
Which dance anew upon the dawn,
Each thundercloud that claps and booms
As rain descends upon the lawn,
And everything that's living
Contains a spark that's sacred, giving
All I see the quality
Of miracles, immense enough for me.

A Thread in Time

I know my time is short,
And ends upon this Earth are ever looming,
But birds are singing,
Flowers blooming,
Rainclouds bringing
Thunder booming,
And sunbeams shining
Down upon my head.
All things I see are intertwining,
And I must write my thoughts before they've fled,
Lest they be lost when time's cut short
And I forget the wonder in each thread.

Alone, with You

The sunset speaks to me,
But I can't quite discern the words.
The circling paths of birds,
Like cursive in the sky, I see
But fail to fully comprehend
The meaning, as their movements blend
With someone singing soft a melody.
Though no one else is near,
That voice is sounding somewhere, clear,
Almost a fantasy.
Each isolated element connected,
My life with something more has intersected,
And suddenly the song is sung by me.

Dimensions Deferred

Are my words constrained
By the number of lines on the page?
Do they shrink to be contained
By those borders, like bars on a cage?
Might your thoughts extend
Beyond what is set up on the stage?
Can imaginations bend
To conform to the structure and gauge
Of the medium where the ideas are spoken?
Or, is the meaning behind every metaphor broken?
Are the passions diluted and stripped of emotion
Like a drop of red wine that is lost in the ocean?
When the depths of the soul are distilled with each word,
What dimensions are dimmed, undefined, or deferred?

The Story in the Paper

I put the pen to paper,
And it seemed to move itself.
A story lived inside the fiber
As real as if it sat upon a shelf.

When the pen was touched to paper,
It awakened something dormant in the page.
A long-lost memory was sleeping –
A forgotten forest where it lived an age.

Before it turned to paper,
It formed the grain that grew beneath the bark
And watched what living things were creeping
Beneath the canopy on soil dark.

Now those remembrances are paper,
A million separate pieces from the trees.
So I will try to put them back together
Before their voices fade upon the breeze.

No Words Tonight

No words tonight,
But yearning pulls my heart.
No progress comes to light
With poems where I've yet to write a part.
But something new is growing,
A wish for more than rhymes that wake the dark
Where stars are glowing
And subtle turns of phrase create a spark.
Desires deeper breach
My simple stanzas, dance beyond my sight
Just barely out of reach,
But still direct my pen to start to write
Without a theme
Save what these lines have just conveyed.
The words arise like steam
And vanish quickly once they've been arrayed.
No words tonight are placed
In spaces where I searched for more,
But still my soul is graced
With something new I'd never thought before.

INDEX OF POEMS

ABOUT THE AUTHOR

John Trimmer was born in Harrisburg, Pennsylvania in 1987. After growing up in the rural, rolling hills of the southern part of the state, he attended Bucknell University in Lewisburg, Pennsylvania. He graduated in 2010 with a Bachelor of Science in Civil and Environmental Engineering. Moving to the University of South Florida, he enrolled in the Civil and Environmental Engineering Department's Peace Corps Master's International Program. From 2011 to 2014, he served as a United States Peace Corps Volunteer in Kalisizo, Uganda, where he worked with Brick by Brick Uganda, an organization focused on local education, economic development, and health. After concluding his service, John returned to the University of South Florida, where he graduated in 2015 with a Master of Science in Environmental Engineering. He then earned a Ph.D. in Environmental Enginerring from the University of Illinois at Urbana-Champaign (UIUC). After spending a year as a post-doctoral researcher at UIUC, he began working with the Aquaya Institute in Nairobi, Kenya, where he leads research focused on improving water safety and sanitation in low-income countries. At the time of this book's publication, he is continuing his work with Aquaya in Kenya.

www.ingramcontent.com/pod-product-compliance
Lightning Source LLC
LaVergne TN
LVHW091209150826
845672LV00005B/1297
* 9 7 9 8 4 1 0 1 7 4 2 1 3 *